Bristol Radical Pamph

The 1963 Bristol Bus Boycott

Silu Pascoe & Joyce Morris-Wisdom

ISBN 978-1-911522-79-9

Bristol Radical History Group. 2024.
www.brh.org.uk
brh@brh.org.uk

There is that great proverb—that until the lions have their own historians, the history of the hunt will always glorify the hunter.

Chinua Achebe, 'The Art of Fiction'
The Paris Review No.139, Winter 1994.

The fight for racial justice

The Bristol Bus Boycott campaign of 1963 is not only part of Bristol's long tradition of campaigning for social justice and equality, but also part of Britain's civil rights movement. It was the first such action of its kind against racial discrimination in employment in post-WW2 Britain. The narrative of the bus boycott has tended to be framed as a campaign for racial justice against the employer, the Bristol Omnibus Company (BOC). However, equally significant was the fact that the activists challenged the racist attitudes and behaviour of a powerful trade union, the Transport and General Workers' Union (TGWU). The campaigners faced a struggle for racial justice on two fronts, both the employer and the trade union, in the context of events not only in Britain but also worldwide, at a time the colour of a person's skin mattered.

The Bristol Bus Boycott campaign has been largely neglected and forgotten by historians. A book of newspaper cuttings in Bristol Central Library's reference section was the main primary source used for this study[1] Newspaper cuttings were also found in the Paul Stephenson Archive created and maintained by himself at Bristol Archives.[2] All sources present various methodological challenges. Newspaper collections come with their own biases as they contain not only the bias of the newspapers but also the bias of the person collecting them. All newspapers have political bias and every journalist is influenced by their conscious and unconscious beliefs. In addition, the collector decides what to omit or include in the collection. National and international newspapers, not included in the collections, were used to supplement local sources.[3] However, tracing the story of the Bristol Bus Boycott through the lens of the predominately white British press of the period, was supplemented by reading documents in various archives.[4] A key secondary source for this study was Madge Dresser's booklet, *Black and White on the Buses: The 1963 Colour Bar Dispute in Bristol.*[5] Originally published in 1986, the pamphlet was the first specific study about this historic event. Recorded memories of black pioneers and conversations with some of the surviving boycott activists have also been upon drawn upon for this study. Oral history can present difficulties as many of the interviews and conversations took place many years after the events that activists were recalling. Giving voice to black perspectives of the Bristol Bus Boycott campaign was important to demonstrate the agency of those who took part.

1 *Coloured Population of Bristol, 1961-1973*—Collection of Newspaper Cuttings. Ref. no. B28496. Location RL2E1.
2 P. Stephenson Archive Papers Collection, Bristol Archives.
3 British newspapers https://www.britishnewspapersarchive.co.uk/titles/
4 Bristol Archive Records https://www.bristolarchiverecords.com
5 Madge Dresser, *Black and White on the Buses: The 1963 Colour Bar Dispute in Bristol* (Bristol Broadsides (Coop) Ltd: 1986, reprinted in 2013).

Note on terminology

Knowing how best to use the language associated with the history of the Bristol Bus Boycott can be complex. Many words used back in the post-WW2 period until the 1960s are now considered offensive. It is important to note that their use in this pamphlet is strictly linked to the historical context, is not deemed appropriate for use today and does not reflect the views of the author. One of these words is 'coloured'. Avtar Brah, in Cartographies of Diaspora: Contesting Identities, has asserted 'coloured' was a term used in Britain in the decades after WW2 to describe migrants from the Caribbean, Africa and South Asia reflecting a colonial vocabulary. It was not a simple descriptive term. It had been the colonial code for a relationship of domination and subordination between coloniser and colonised. In the metropolis of Britain, the term went along with racist practices of stigmatisation, inferiority, exclusion and/or discrimination, in areas such as employment, education, housing, the media, the criminal justice service, immigration and health services.

Background context — Britain

Initially, immigrants from Europe were encouraged to settle and work in British cities in the post-WW2 boom. Britain recruited Polish ex-servicemen and European voluntary workers from refugee camps and from Italy.[6] However, continuing labour shortages in the 1950s led British officials to encourage New Commonwealth ie African, Caribbean and Asian migrants to come and fill the gaps. Initially, many saw themselves as migrants as they aimed to spend two to five years in Britain, in order to get training or earn enough money to live on and return home again. However, many did not return to their homelands but became residents, giving up their place in their own national history in order to play a role in the history of Britain. This is the group commonly known as the 'Windrush Generation' which refers to the group of Caribbean migrants who came to the UK between 1948 and the early 1970s. Legally, they were not immigrants but British citizens. The 1948 Nationality Act created a single category of citizenship, that of 'British Subject: citizen of the UK and Colonies'

6 W. Sullivan, 'Black Workers and Trade Unions 1945-2000' in *Britain at Work: Voices from the workplace 1915-1995*. TUC Library Collections, 2012.

for persons belonging not just to the UK itself, but also to any place which was still a British colony on 1st January 1949. This had the effect of ensuring that people from British colonies in the Caribbean and elsewhere had a legal right to come to the UK to live and work. The great majority of Caribbean settlers were in their 20s, and usually the jobs they were offered were those that local people didn't want, even though a quarter of the men and half the women were non-manual workers. Peter Fryer described them as "willing black hands [who] drove tube trains, collected bus fares and emptied hospital patients' bed-pans".[7] and Nicholas Deakin commented, "They took their citizenship seriously and many regarded themselves, not as strangers, but as kinds of Englishmen. Everything taught in school … encouraged this belief".[8]

However, though half of Britain's white population had never even met a black person and among those who had, the acquaintance had mostly been casual, prejudice against black people was widespread.[9] Housing, education and employment were the crucial problems facing black migrants. In housing, an overt colour bar was advertised, 'No Blacks, No Irish, No Dogs'. In education, black children were taught the history and culture of a white society by a white teacher, learning little or nothing of the society and culture from which they and their parents originated. This implied an 'inferiority' or 'backwardness' of their cultural background. By favouring the teaching of British history without its black and Asian contributions, the British Empire was legitimised, thus maintaining and sustaining racist stereotypes about black and Asian people. Increasing numbers of black children, especially black boys, were excluded from mainstream schools and sent to schools which were then called Educationally Subnormal Schools.[10]

Racial discrimination and racial prejudice in employment were steeply entrenched. In many industries, white trade unionists resisted the employment of black workers (effectively a colour bar) or insisted on a 'colour quota' system. Recruitment of black workers was limited to a token handful, generally about 5%.[11] Often there was an "understanding with managements that the hallowed rule of 'last in, first out' should not apply to whites when coloured immigrants are employed and that coloured workers shall not be promoted over white".[12] With craft unions, a Jamaican clerical worker summed up the situation as "Union: 'Get a job and we will give you membership' and Employer: 'Join the union and you will get a job'".[13]

7 Peter Fryer, *Staying Power: The History of Black People in Britain* (London: Pluto Press, 1984) p.373.
8 Nicholas Deakin et al, *Colour Citizenship and British Society* (London: Panther Books, 1970) p.283.
9 Peter Fryer, p.374
10 B. Coard, *How the West Indian Child is made Educationally Sub-Normal in the British School System* (New Beacon Books, 1971)
11 P. Fryer, *Staying Power*, p.376.
12 *The Times*, 9 November 1954, p.9.
13 R.B. Davison *'Commonwealth Immigrants'* (London: OUP, 1964) p.70.

Black migrant workers came to Britain, essentially for economic reasons, expecting trade unions to uphold their rights and privileges and to protect their interests like all other workers. They were accustomed to the ideas and practices of trade unionism in their home countries. The growing grievances of black workers in the workplace posed a challenge to the British trade union movement and its beliefs in equality and the 'Brotherhood of Man'. It was the acid test of the British trade union movement to implement its 'Brotherhood of Man' ideal for black workers in 'the Mother Country'. Before 1955, there was no reference either in the Trade Union Congress (TUC) General Council[14] report or during the Annual Congress proceedings to 'race relations', racial discrimination or immigration in relation to Britain.

However, the 1955 TUC Congress was instructive. While, in principle, it condemned racial discrimination or colour prejudice, it nevertheless implicitly accepted the 'problem' was not the expression of prejudice or discriminatory practice by white employers and workers but was attributable to the very presence of immigrants from the Caribbean. The TUC argued during the 1950s and 1960s that black workers did not integrate with white workers. This helped to stereotype black migrant workers as a 'problem' and 'other'.[15]

By the end of 1957, there was no clear and positive response from the TUC to the claim that black workers were subjected to the prejudice and discrimination of white workers. The view prevailed that it was the responsibility of the New Commonwealth immigrants to take action against racism.[16] Significantly, after the 'riots' in Nottingham and London's Notting Hill in 1958, the General Council issued a statement at the TUC annual conference that the official policy was opposed to racial discrimination:

> The Trade Union movement has been forthright in its condemnation
> of every manifestation of racial prejudice and discrimination in any
> part of the world. Here in Britain, immigrants from many countries
> have been freely accepted into membership of trade unions and, in
> general, have been integrated into industrial life.[17]

Many individual unions and branches submitted similar resolutions denouncing discrimination. Within the trade union movement, there was

---

14 The TUC is a national federation of trade unions that collectively represent most unionised workers in England and Wales. The TUC's decision-making body is the Annual Congress. The TUC General Council represents the variety of unions represented within the TUC. The General Council presents a report of their work during the previous year to the TUC Congress for their approval.
15 W. Sullivan *Black Workers* p.2.
16 R.Ramdin *The Making of The Black Working Class in Britain* (Hants: Gower Publishing Company Ltd: 1987), p.345.
17 Report of the Proceedings of the 90th Annual TUC Sept 1958, p.459.

a disparity of views, reflected in the approach of policy-makers and the attitudes and behaviour at other levels of the organisation. In reality, as the 'high command' in trade unions passed resolutions deploring colour prejudice, some local branches operated 'colour bars' and 'colour quotas'. There was no united approach on the employment of 'coloured' workers among the local branches of any one trade union. This was particularly demonstrated with the Transport and General Workers' Union (TGWU) in relation to the Bristol Bus Boycott, as will be detailed later when the situation in Bristol is explained.

Ambiguous attitudes towards black workers existed within the trade union movement. Trade unionists were simultaneously asking black workers to join trade unions, but also calling for a ban on black immigration to Britain. They feared that black workers would undercut white workers' wages—because they would be paid less and opportunities for overtime earnings would be reduced—and weaken agreements; that employers would use them as a pool of cheap, sweated labour; and use them as 'blacklegs' in the event of strikes.[18] These arguments of white workers against black workers were rooted in the fear of economic competition and the racist legacy of colonialism. During the 1950s and 1960s, trade unions were at the height of their power and had enormous potential to effect radical change for the benefit of their black and Asian members. However, the difference between the rhetoric and practice of the trade union movement meant it failed in its duty of care towards its black and Asian members.

As the numbers of black and Asian migrants increased, the Labour government of 1945–1951, came under pressure from its own MPs to curb immigration. However, it concluded that a very large increase in migration in the future might make legislation for control essential but this was not justified at the current time.[19]

The word 'immigrant' was negatively stigmatizing, denying British citizens of 'colour' the citizenship they were entitled to by law. A persistent theme in British history is the use of immigration policies as a solution to fix the country's socio-economic problems. The state essentially problematizes the presence of black people in Britain by introducing immigration legislation.

The following Conservative government actively sought to introduce immigration legislation. Community organisations led the campaign against this. Umbrella groups formed, combining black organisations with sympathetic white groups, to campaign against the 1962 Commonwealth Immigrants Bill. The most prominent of these organisations were the Birmingham-based Coordinating Committee Against Racial Discrimination and the Conference

---

18 Blacklegs is a pejorative term for strikebreakers, ie people who work despite a strike.
19 Cabinet Papers, 1951 Immigration of British Subjects into the United Kingdom, CP 128/44, February, TNA.

of Afro-Asian-Caribbean Organisations in London.[20] However, the campaigns did not stop the bill as the first Commonwealth Immigrants Act became law in 1962. This Act basically reversed the 1948 British Nationality Act. The right to migration to Britain guaranteed to all Commonwealth citizens was effectively revoked. Certain provisions transformed resident black citizens into immigrants, subject to surveillance and deportation. Serious inroads were made into the civil rights of British citizens whose passports had been issued outside the UK. They were now subject to entry control.[21]

The 1962 Act was a piece of discriminatory legislation with the obvious intention to reduce the total annual inflow of black people into Britain. Its unstated and unrecognised assumption was that the mere presence of black people was the source of a problem in Britain. Official policy responses to perceived 'problems' of integration reflected prevailing attitudes to 'race relations'.[22] Ironically, in the run up to the implementation of 1962 Act, more wives and families came to Britain to join their husbands and fathers, to beat the impending legislation.[23] By doing so, they moved from immigrant to settler status.

International context

The problem of the 20th Century is the problem of the color-line—the relation of the darker to the lighter races of men in Asia and Africa, in America and the islands of the sea.

W.E.B. Du Bois.[24]

The matter of the colour of a person's skin was already an internationally sensitive issue by the late 1950s. It featured in the daily news from Africa, Asia, the Caribbean and America.

By 1963, many anti-colonial/anti-imperialist struggles in Africa, Asia and the Caribbean had resulted in independence for a significant number of countries. However, national liberation movements were still active, especially in Africa. The National Liberation Movement in South Africa had particular significance for Britain, as the Nationalist government of 1948 had implemented an official 'apartheid' system, a racially discriminatory system

20 W. Sullivan, *Black Workers* p.1.
21 P. Fryer, *Staying Power*, p.382.
22 K. Hammond Perry *London is the Place for Me* (Oxford: Oxford University Press, 2015).
23 D. Dabydeen, J. Gilmore & C. Jones (eds) *The Oxford Companion to Black British History* (Oxford: Oxford University Press, 2007) p.498.
24 W.E.B. Du Bois *The Souls of Black Folk* (London: Penguin,1996) p13.

whereby different categories of citizens were subject to different laws and policies depending on their skin colour. It is important to understand this context as it had an impact within Britain in general, and on the Bristol Bus Boycott campaign, in particular.

There were precedents for a black-led bus boycott campaign as a form of protest against racial discrimination. South Africa saw its first in 1957. During 1956 and early 1957, the main transport company on the Witwatersrand, the Public Utility Transport Company (PUTCO), announced increases in fares of one penny on a four-penny bus ride. To black people, this attack on their miserably inadequate wages was intolerable and it was decided to boycott the buses. 'Azikwelwa' ('they shall not be ridden'), became the cry in Johannesburg's vast African townships of Alexandra, and Sophiatown and in Randfontein in Pretoria. From January to June 1957, 70,000 men and women walked to work and back, ten miles each way, rather than pay an increase in fares imposed by the privately-owned bus company. The government tried to break the boycott by police harassment and intimidation. The employers became anxious when the boycotters threatened to stop walking to work and to stay at home. After many months, PUTCO dropped the proposed fare increase. Employers agreed to pay a transport levy and the government undertook to subsidise PUTCO. *The New Age* newspaper reported on its front page, "This is one of the most remarkable illustrations of African solidarity ever to be witnessed in this country".[25]

The struggle to end apartheid became international in the form of the Anti-Apartheid Movement. In 1993, Oliver Tambo remarked, "The AAM grew into perhaps the strongest international solidarity movement of the 20th century, bringing together citizens of all countries, governments and international organisations".[26]

The Anti-Apartheid Movement in Britain campaigned against apartheid in both South Africa and Namibia. Outside London, the Bristol Anti-Apartheid group was one of the largest and most active in the country.[27]

The civil rights movement in America

The birth of the American civil rights movement (CRM) owed much to events happening elsewhere in the world. As Martin Luther King Jr. commented, "The Negro had watched the decolonization and liberation of nations in Africa

25 ANC *From Unity in Action: A Photographic History of the ANC, South Africa 1912-1982* (London: ANC, 1982), p96. New Age. volume 3 Feb 1957.
26 Oliver Tambo, ANC President, opening speech at the International Solidarity Conference on the theme "From Peace, Democracy and Development", 19 February 1993.
27 Bristol Anti-Apartheid Archives are filed in Bristol Archives.

and Asia since WW2".[28] Between the years 1954 and 1965,[29] the movement employed a range of tactics including bus boycotts, petitions, marches and sit-ins in its struggle against racial injustice and for equal rights for all. The US CRM was important because it provided a potent protest model for non-white people in Britain—non-violent direct action.

Lasting 381 days, the most well-known bus boycott of the US CRM was the Montgomery Bus Boycott which started on 1st December 1955 when Rosa Parks refused to give up her seat on a bus so a white person could sit down. She was arrested and initially detained at the local jail. E.D. Nixon, a past president of the local and state National Association for the Advancement of Coloured People (NAACP), and Jo Ann Robinson, Women's Political Council president, saw the opportunity of making Rosa Park's arrest a test case and rallying point for a community-wide boycott of the bus system. In a radio interview in 1956, Rosa Parks famously said, "I had decided that I would have to know, once and for all, what rights I had as a human being, and a citizen?"[30]

The Montgomery Improvement Association was established to organise the boycott and Martin Luther King was selected to lead it. It had four demands centred around ending legally-required segregation on the buses and improving the treatment of black passengers. However, the fourth demand was the hiring of black drivers on predominately black routes. On 4th June 1956, a three-judge federal district court handed down its majority decision in a case brought by four Montgomery black women to end bus segregation in the city:

> We hold that the statutes requiring segregation of the white and coloured races on a common carrier violate the due process and equal protection clauses of the 14th Amendment.[31]

Montgomery officials appealed the case to the US Supreme Court and on 13th November 1956, the Court affirmed the decision of the lower court in declaring Alabama's state local laws requiring segregation on buses to be unconstitutional. The four black women had successfully used the law to effect change, as it was the courts that ended segregation on the buses.

In all of the above political struggles, women, especially black women, played an active role. Black women suffered a three-fold oppression: as black people, as women and as workers who largely formed an army of poorly

28 Martin Luther King, Jr, *Why We Can't Wait* (New York: Harper and Row, 1964).
29 J. Williams *Eyes on the Prize America's Civil Rights Years, 1954-1965* (New York: Viking Penguin Inc, 1987).
30 Rosa Parks's radio interview with Sydney Rogers in West Oakland 1956. Cited in C Marsh *The Beloved Community: How Faith Shapes Social Justice from the Civil Rights to Today* (New York: Basic Books, 2006), p.21.
31 Ref Browder v Gayle 142F Supp 707 MD. Ala. 1956 Justia US Law.

paid labour of low status. Women were active both in areas in which women, through their own organisations, mounted campaigns themselves and in the campaigns of organisations embracing both women and men, in which the participation of women was vital. They have been the unsung heroines in the struggles for racial and social justice, including the Bristol Bus Boycott. Comparison can be drawn between the Bristol Bus Boycott campaign and the civil rights campaigns elsewhere in the world. References were made to the wider global context throughout the boycott campaign. The bus boycott in Bristol exposed the hypocrisy of Britain's position as a country condemning other nations whilst upholding a 'colour bar' of their own in employment and racially discriminating against black people in every aspect of their lives.

Bristol

The year 1963 became a watershed moment in the British civil rights movement. Growing numbers of Commonwealth migrants had moved to live in Bristol in the early 1960s. In 1961, an estimated 3,000 residents were of African-Caribbean origin,[32] some of whom had served in the British military during WW2 and some of whom had emigrated to Britain since then. Since the 1950s, a large number of them have lived in the areas of Easton, St. Jude's and St. Paul's. They experienced racial discrimination in housing, employment, education and social welfare. They also encountered endemic and overt everyday racism from white people. The booklet, *Our History Many Rivers to Cross* by the Malcolm X Elders Forum gave explicit examples of their experiences in Bristol during this period: "We are the people who overcame racial abuse, religious ridicule and financial hardship".[33]

Bus Boycott activists remembered similar experiences during this period. Roy Hackett recalled during the 50th anniversary of the campaign that, "There was so much racism about".[34] Guy Bailey commented that, "Black teenagers would walk around in groups for safety. We weren't able to go anywhere without meeting violent Teddy Boys. I was chased by them on more than one occasion".[35]

In response to the racism, the black community set up their own churches, clubs and associations. The West Indian Association (WIA), formed in 1957, had begun to act as a representative body. Its chair, Bill Smith, knew local Labour councillors, most notably, Wally Jenkins, who represented the St Paul's area and also TGWU officials.

32 By 1963, an estimate of 7,000 residents were of African-Caribbean origin.
33 The Malcolm X Elders Forum *Our History Many Rivers to Cross* Bristol Community Education Service.
34 www.bristol.bristolarchiverecords.com/people/people_roy_hackett.html
35 Guy Bailey at 'An Evening with Guy Bailey' on 28 August 2023. People's Republic of Stokes Croft.

In 1962, unhappy about the lack of progress in fighting racial discrimination by the WIA, which adopted a gradualist approach to change, four young African-Caribbean men, Roy Hackett, Owen Henry, Audley Evans and Prince Brown formed an action group, later to be called the West Indian Development Council (WIDC).

One of the foremost grievances of black people in Bristol was the 'colour bar' operated by the Bristol Omnibus Company (BOC). Despite there being a reported labour shortage on the buses, the bus company refused to employ black and Asian workers as bus crew (ie conductors and drivers) in the city. In the 1960s, Bristol bus services were operated by Bristol Joint Services which was jointly owned by the Corporation of Bristol (Bristol City Council) and the Bristol Omnibus Company, and overseen by the Corporation's Joint Transport Committee (JTC).

Privately owned Bristol Omnibus Company had a 'closed shop' agreement with the TGWU, that is, being a member of the union was a requirement of being employed by the company. Founded in 1922, the TGWU had become the biggest union in the country by the late 1930s. Its first general secretary was Ernest Bevin, who incidentally had, at one point, been a conductor on Bristol's horse-trams. This powerful trade union represented many thousands of bus workers across Britain.

Roy Hackett and Owen Henry had seen black people working on the buses in other major cities. Owen Henry reasoned that:

> although there was no black crews in any of the (Bristol) buses … there was quite enough black people that were using the buses … enough to pay a black person's wages and this wasn't being done.[36]

In the late 1950s, the BOC colour bar's existence was known about but not challenged by either the council or the local leadership of the TGWU.[37] It seems that BOC introduced the ban after a union ballot of workers in 1955, an accusation which local union officials denied, blaming the bus company for operating the colour bar.

However, at this time, the TGWU branch in Bristol did not operate coherently or consistently within national policy or even amongst its own membership within the bus company. The 'Passenger Group' of the local branch which represented drivers and conductors who directly served the public passed a resolution in 1955 that 'coloured workers' should not be employed as bus crews. In contrast, the maintenance section of the same

36 Madge Dresser, *Black and White on the Buses: The 1963 Colour Bar Dispute in Bristol* (Bristol Broadsides (Co-op) Ltd: 1986) p.13.
37 M. Dresser, *Black and White* p.12.

branch, representing members whose role it was to upkeep and repair the buses, voted the other way.[38] Black workers were therefore employed in lower paid positions in the bus company's workshops, garages and canteens but not as drivers or conductors.

Andrew Hake, a curate attached to the Bishop of Bristol's Industrial Mission recalled that, "The TGWU in the city, had said that if one black man steps on the platform as a conductor, every wheel will stop".[39] Hake confronted a member of the management of BOC on this issue sometime in 1956 or 1957. The management, he recalls, told him:

> [they had] no objection to employing black people ... but [that] the unions had made their position clear and the management were not prepared to face a showdown, a confrontation which would have led to strike action. And so they were biding their time and waiting for this to change.[40]

By the early 1960s, one local Labour activist, then a Bristol Trades Council member, confirmed that:

> It was taken for granted in the movement that the TGWU was operating a veto ... one could not help but notice there wasn't a single coloured face [on the buses] ... apart from some we never saw who might be washing down the things at night.[41]

The *Bristol Evening Post* ran a series of articles about racial discrimination in 1961. One article, written by Malcolm Smith, revealed there was "a flat refusal by the undermanned BOC to employ coloured people in their crews, however high their skill".[42] The company blamed colour prejudice amongst the workers as the reason for the lack of black employees. Smith also revealed, "it has been alleged that in Bristol, there is a colour bar among local members of the TGWU".[43] Ron Nethercott, the TGWU's regional secretary, adamantly denied any decision had been made to ban black workers, saying, "there is no colour bar. We have a lot of coloured members in Bristol, most of them on the labouring side".[44] The bus company's general manager, Ian Patey, reportedly explained, "A few West Indians were employed in the garage but this was

38 *Bristol Evening Post* 2 May 1963 p.18.
39 M. Dresser, *Black and White*, A Hake interview, p.12.
40 M. Dresser, *Black and White*, A Hake interview, p.13.
41 M. Dresser, *Black and White*, D. Bateman interview, p.13.
42 *Bristol Evening Post* 1 November 1961.
43 *Bristol Evening Post* 1 November 1961.
44 *Bristol Evening Post* 1 November 1961.

labouring work in which capacity most employers were prepared to accept them".[45] Malcolm Smith's article concluded that a formal colour bar probably did exist on the buses, despite the denials of both union and management.

In February 1962, Ian Patey was invited to attend a mid-March session of the Joint Transport Committee (JTC), where he justified the colour bar. He said that he had "factual evidence" that the introduction of coloured crews in other cities downgraded the job and caused existing white staff to go elsewhere.[46] The JTC decided after some discussion, not to oppose the company's colour bar. The principal excuse given against employing black people on Bristol's buses was that they would reduce overtime for current employees. Pay was low and workers relied on overtime to make ends meet. In order to get a living wage, there actually needed to be a shortage of staff to provide the chance for overtime.

By labelling the reasons as economic, people tried to distance their views from being racist. However, regardless of economic considerations, discrimination in any shape or form on the basis of skin colour was still racist. A secondary reason given, one that exposed the racism, was that 'coloured' employees were a danger to female white conductresses and passengers.[47] In 1963, the chairman of BOC said that,

> If we did start employing coloured people while we can still get white people, a lot of these white females would be leaving the job to go and get other jobs in the city.[48]

In 2013, fifty years after the bus boycott, Tony Fear, a white driver, recalled the racist prejudices held in the company at the time:

> The worst were the conductresses, I have to say. They were terrible. They'd say a black conductor would eventually become a driver, therefore they'd have to work with a black driver, and the things they could do at the end of the journey, you know? It was terrible. They thought they were wide open to rape. They believed that.[49]

In 1962, Roy Hackett's wife, Ena Hackett, applied for a job as a bus conductress and was turned down. Years later, Roy Hackett, in an interview with Madge Dresser, commented:

45 *Bristol Evening Post* 1 November 1961.
46 Minutes of the Joint Transport Committee (Bristol Corporation) 15 March 1962, para 1371.
47 *Bristol Evening Post* 2 May 1963.
48 T. Mazumdar, 'What was behind Bristol bus boycott?', *Newsnight*, 28 August 2013.
49 J. Kelly, 'What was behind the Bristol bus boycott of 1963?', *BBC News*, 27 August 2013.

it always been in the newspaper, the *Evening Post* that, "we cannot run the buses because we haven't got any staff." And at the time my wife had applied for a job on the buses. Unfortunately, it was always, "No, we can't have you." Then there was no law against discrimination.[50]

Discrimination on the basis of skin colour was absolutely legal at that time and the BOC was acting within its rights to operate a colour bar in employment. However, Roy Hackett, Owen Henry and Audley Evans were determined to do something about the situation. They argued, "Well, it's about time to put pressure on Bristol City Council." We thought, "should we talk to them?—Yes! We sent a delegation to the BCC telling them of our plight ... before the [1963] crisis, through Bill Smith. And we never get anywhere and we thought it's about time for action".[51]

The small group of activists who later formed the WIDC decided to launch a campaign for equal rights to employment on the city's buses. They chose Paul Stephenson as their spokesman, a young man who in 1962 had arrived in Bristol as the city's first black youth and community development officer and a supply teacher. He saw the bus issue as one that "would bring out racism"[52] and reflected in his memoirs that:

I decided to take on the Bristol Bus Company, because it was a symbol of all that was wrong with Bristol, as it advocated racism, defended racism and was the most notorious racist employer in the city.[53]

Paul Stephenson was British-born to a West African father and Black British mother. He recognised that it was a civil rights issue and explained that,

In my own life experience, though I was completely English, my colour made me realise that there were no rights for black people, no legal protection from discrimination and injustice.[54]

He set up a test case to prove that a 'colour bar' existed in the BOC's employment policy. He arranged an interview with the bus company for Guy Bailey, an 18-year-old night-school student of his, who had impeccable credentials. Guy Bailey reported:

50 M. Dresser, *Black and White*, R. Hackett interview, p.14.
51 M. Dresser, *Black and White*, p.14.
52 M. Dresser, *Black and White*, P. Stephenson interview, p.15.
53 P. Stephenson and L. Morrison, *Memoirs of A Black Englishman* (Bristol: Tangent Books, 2011) p.51.
54 Stephenson and Morrison, p.5.

I turned up dressed in my blazer and a nice tie and shirt. The receptionist looked a bit surprised and said, "Can I help you?". I said that I was here for the interview and she said, "No, we're expecting a Mr. Guy Bailey." I said that was me. She called through to the manager and said," The two o'clock is here, but he's black." I heard him say back, "Tell him all the vacancies are filled".[55]

On learning from Guy Bailey that he had been refused an interview, Paul Stephenson took him the next day to meet with Ian Patey, the general manager of the company. Mr Patey confirmed that the bus company did not employ black workers. In his memoirs, Paul Stephenson recounted Ian Patey's reaction to him declaring that the WIDC would take action against the colour bar. Patey said, "go away with your campaign, we are not employing black people".[56] Guy Bailey recalled that Ian Patey "told us to leave, if not, he would call the police".[57] As Guy Bailey and Paul Stephenson were members of the TGWU, they then visited the local head office in Transport House (now Tony Benn House) seeking support but were given no help from the union.[58] It is questionable whether the TGWU head office knew of the Passenger Group policy or knew about it but was turning a blind eye.

Inspired by Rosa Parks and the Montgomery Bus Boycott, Paul Stephenson and the other WIDC activists decided on a bus boycott campaign in Bristol. Paul Stephenson called a press conference on 29th April 1963 to announce their action. Owen Henry was photographed by the local press, standing 'at the back of the bus'. He later explained that this was where bus conductors stood. For him, it was symbolic defiance of racial segregation—Bristol style. By identifying with the US CRM, black citizens in Bristol were by extension comparing the British authorities to their American South counterparts who legally enforced segregation. The announcement of the boycott, also exposed the hypocrisy of the local trade union, for, as Paul Stephenson asked:

How can a union be prepared to support a boycott of South African goods, [and] refuse to do anything about racial prejudice on its own doorstep?[59]

The basic premise was a call for black and Asian Bristolians and white allies to stay off the buses and use other forms of transport. The bus boycott

55 *Socialist Worker* interview with Guy Bailey. 8 October 2013.
56 P. Stephenson and L. Morrison *Memoirs*. p.52.
57 In conversation with Guy Bailey on 21 November 2023.
58 In conversation with Guy Bailey on 21 November 2023.
59 *Bristol Evening Post*, 30 April 1963.

Left—Guy Bailey, the young man who sparked the Bristol Bus Boycott.

Top-right—From left to right, Audley Evans, Paul Stephenson, and Owen Henry discuss the campaign, 30th April 1963.

Bottom-right—Students and WIDC activists march in support of the bus boycott.

Top—Picketing at the bus station.

Bottom—One of the many placards used in the campaign.

activism included public speeches, pickets of the bus depots, blockades, sit downs, petitions and protest marches. All these activities contributed to mounting pressure on the company and trade union to lift the colour bar. However, unlike in the Montgomery Bus Boycott campaign, Bristol's black population did not have sufficient numbers required to bring the company to its knees through the removal of their custom. Paul Stephenson realised that the bus boycott itself would need to be part of a wider campaign strategy to challenge the 'institutional racism'[60] of both the employer and the TGWU local branch.

Paul Stephenson recognised that press attention was key to raising public awareness and gaining support for the campaign. He cannily invited the local press to the public launch of the bus boycott campaign on 29th April 1963. Press cuttings show that there was regular coverage by the local newspapers, the *Bristol Evening Post* and *Western Daily Press*, especially over the initial two-week period. The campaign also caught the attention of some of the major national dailies. The proposed boycott got front page coverage in the Jamaican newspaper, *The Gleaner*, and Claudia Jones also covered the story in her paper, *The West Indian Gazette*.[61] Stephenson later commented that, "The press had a mixed reaction to us but their discussion about the boycott in both local and national press kept our campaign in the public eye".[62]

Analysis of the newspaper coverage of the Bristol Bus Boycott campaign was very instructive with regard to how news was manufactured during that period. On 30th April, the *Bristol Evening Post* front page headline declared, "W.Indians 100pc for Bus Boycott".[63] Joyce Morris-Wisdom commented that the press inadvertently helped the campaign as the headline provoked a response from the black community who came out in support in great numbers.[64] Photos can create blind spots in cultural memory, especially with historical events like the Bristol Bus Boycott, when only certain things were deemed worthy to photograph and appear in the white media of that time. There was very little photographic newspaper evidence of black people engaged in the marches, sit-ins and picketing. In contrast, the students' march, with WIDC members, on 1st May 1963, received widespread coverage with photos and articles in local newspapers and also film footage on television news. The

---

60 Sir W. Macpherson's definition of institutional racism: 'The collective failure of an organisation to provide an appropriate and professional service to people because of their colour, culture or ethnic origin.' *The Stephen Lawrence Inquiry: Report of an inquiry by Sir William Macpherson* (Home Office CM 4262-1 Published 24 February 1999).
61 Coloured population of Bristol, 1961-1973—Collection of Newspaper Cuttings. Ref.no.B28496 Bristol Reference Library.
62 Stephenson and Morrison, p.57.
63 *Bristol Evening Post* 30 April 1963.
64 In conversation with Joyce Morris-Wisdom on 28 April 2023.

few photos included in newspaper articles were mainly of Paul Stephenson and occasionally some of the other WIDC leaders. Paul Stephenson became the public face of the bus boycott campaign in the press.

When the local reporters questioned the bus company about the boycott, the general manager, Ian Patey, vigorously defended the racist employment policy. He said, "The company's policy regarding coloured labour had been clear for years and the action by the West Indians would not make them reconsider their policy".[65]

An *Evening Post* editorial pointed out that to justify a colour bar because of the prejudice that coloured labour would arouse had an "unhappy ring of convenience." However, in the same editorial, the *Post* also questioned the union which represented the workers:

> What are the trade union leaders doing to get the race virus out of the systems of their rank and file … The union has had plenty to say about South Africa. They should take a look nearer home.[66]

The TGWU officials were not pleased at being attacked by the press in public. They resented Stephenson's approaching them *after* the boycott was announced. They consequently refused to meet a deputation from the WIDC.[67] Arthur Coxwell of the local TGWU had reportedly made it clear in a letter to Stephenson that:

> The union had no colour bar and that the decision not to employ West Indians had been made by the Bus Company alone.[68]

On 1st May, traditionally a day which is celebrated worldwide as Workers' Day, over a hundred students from Bristol University, with the WIDC, held a protest march from the Victoria Rooms, down Park Street to the bus station and then to the local HQ of the TGWU at Transport House, Victoria Street. This march attracted heckling from bus crews. Their actions were later reported on the front page of *Nonesuch* News, the student union newsletter:

> At the bus station, a vigil was held and several lively discussions took place with employees of the company. After the vigil, the march went to the HQ of the TGWU, where a letter of protest was handed in. During the following week, students collected signatures for a

65 *Bristol Evening Post* 30 April 1963.
66 *Bristol Evening Post* 30 April 1963.
67 M. Dresser, p.20.
68 *Bristol Evening Post* 1 May 1963.

petition to the bus company. This was handed in a week after the march with 2,114 names attached.[69]

The university students recognised that both the union and bus company were responsible for the situation. An article in the autumn edition of their termly *Nonesuch Magazine* (a subsidiary of their weekly *Nonesuch News*) stated, "At the height of the controversy, it was repeatedly made clear that the people were protesting at the unions, as well as the company".[70]

Ron Nethercott was apparently "furious" and told the marchers:

> We don't want discrimination and we don't like it. There is no question of a colour bar as far as we are concerned. Without consulting the Regional Committee, I am prepared to say that if there are coloured workers on the buses, our people will accept them.[71]

This claim was undermined when on the day after the protest march, Nethercott and the union's Regional Chairman, Desmond Brown, went to meet the Town Clerk and representatives of the Jamaican High Commission. That same evening the banner headlines in the *Evening Post* read:

BRISTOL BUS CREW BACK THE BOSS[72]

The next morning, the *Western Daily Press* headline quoted the busmen's declaration:

WE WON'T WORK WITH WEST INDIANS[73]

In the days that followed, Owen Henry and Paul Stephenson made speeches, especially in an effort to win over newly arrived migrants who did not want to rock the boat.[74] Owen Henry was very well respected within the St Paul's community. He helped many fellow black residents with the immigration paperwork necessary to enable their dependents, left in the Caribbean, to join them in Bristol.[75]

Roy Hackett organised marches and sit-down protests to block roads in key areas around the bus depot and the city centre, so no buses could enter

---

69 *Nonesuch News* 17 May 1963.
70 *Nonesuch Magazine* Autumn 1963 edition.
71 *Bristol Evening Post* 2 May 1963.
72 *Bristol Evening Post* 2 May 1963.
73 *Western Daily Press* 3 May 1963.
74 P. Stephenson and L. Morrison *Memoirs*, p.54.
75 In conversation with Joyce Montague on the Bristol Bus Boycott Guided Walk, 30 September 2023.

or leave. At an interview for the 50th anniversary of the boycott, Roy Hackett recalled,

> We had a lot of help from white people. There were students and a lot of women. They'd drop the kids at school then come and chat to us.[76]

In 2020, he commented that the whole campaign was based on non-violent direct action.[77] Hackett reported, "I said to everyone, not one stick and not one stone".[78] Guy Bailey also emphasised that, "support for the boycott didn't just come from West Indians. We felt supported by white people too. It was encouraging".[79]

Paul Stephenson gained major publicity coups by enlisting the political support of Bristol Labour MPs Tony Benn[80] and Stan Awbery, plus Sir Learie Constantine and Laurence Lindo, the High Commissioners of Trinidad and Tobago and of Jamaica, where the majority of Bristol Caribbean settlers came from. Tony Benn declared his early support for the boycott by saying, "I shall stay off the buses, even if I have to find a bike!"[81] Benn recalled in his memoirs that Desmond Brown of the Bristol TGWU phoned him to criticise him for jumping on the bandwagon and supporting the boycott. By 5th May 1963, Benn's discussions with Ron Nethercott and other union members caused him to be critical of the union's response to the boycott. He wrote in his diary,

> I can't stand the equivocation and hypocrisy of pretending this is caused by "troublemakers", as of course the union was maintaining.[82]

Tony Benn gave more active support to the campaign by contacting the then Labour Party opposition leader, Harold Wilson, who spoke out in support of the boycott and against the colour bar.

On 2nd May 1963, the *Evening Post* headline proclaimed:

NOW WILSON JOINS THE COLOUR BAR FRAY[83]

Wilson told an anti-apartheid rally in London that:

---

76 *Socialist Worker* interview with Roy Hackett 8 October 2013.
77 K. Andrews interview with Roy Hackett. *The Guardian* 6 August 2020.
78 T. Mazumdar 'What was behind Bristol bus boycott?', *Newsnight*, 28 August 2013.
79 A conversation with Guy Bailey on 21 November 2023.
80 Tony Benn was both a member of the TGWU and shadow (opposition) Minister for Transport.
81 *Bristol Evening Post* 2 May 1963.
82 T. Benn *Out of the Wilderness Diaries*, 1963-1967 (London: Hutchison, 1987), p.14.
83 *Bristol Evening Post* 3 May 1963.

The last example of the colour bar (in Britain) is now being operated by the BOC. I'm so glad that so many Bristolians are supporting the campaign to get it abolished. We wish them every success.[84]

Tony Benn later revealed that the Bristol Bus Boycott had finally helped to convince Harold Wilson of the need for race relations legislation.[85]

Paul Stephenson recalled in his memoirs the support that he received from Wilson in publicly condemning the racist employment policy of BOC. His first personal meeting with him was at a House of Commons dinner given for the leaders of the immigrant Caribbean community. Stephenson recounted, "He [Harold Wilson] promised that he would introduce laws against racial discrimination if he became Prime Minister".[86]

Labour MP Stan Awbery, a TGWU member and former organiser, compared the unfolding situation to South Africa by declaring, "We don't want apartheid in Bristol".[87] He handed in a question to Ernest Marples, Transport Secretary, asking if he was aware that racial policies were still being operated by some bus companies. Awbery was told by Marples, "I do not think that the road transport licensing machinery would be appropriate for this purpose. I would, however, expect road transport operations to avoid racial discrimination in their employment policy".[88]

On 2nd May 1963, Labour Party Alderman Henry Henessey spoke of the apparent collusion between bus company and the local TGWU over the 'colour bar'.[89] This was significant as he was a member of the Joint Transport Committee. On 3rd May, the ruling Labour group on the city council threatened him with expulsion, despite his honourable service of over 40 years.[90] The response of the Eastville bus crews to Labour Party involvement was to threaten a walk out if black labour was employed and they expected full support from Bristol's eight other bus depots to "withhold their voluntary contribution to Labour Party funds as a protest against yesterday's intervention by Mr Harold Wilson and Mr A.W. Benn".[91]

After the local TGWU branch's refusal to meet with a WIDC delegation, an increasingly bitter war of words was fought out in the local press. A game of political 'pass the parcel' ensued between the BOC and TGWU. In addition, public sentiment was further inflamed on 3rd May, when the two local TV

84 *Western Daily Press* 3 May1963.
85 P Mason *Learie Constantine* (Oxford: Signal Books, 2008), p.158.
86 P. Stephenson and L. Morrison *Memoirs*, p.56.
87 *Bristol Evening Post* 3 May 1963.
88 Road Transport Operators (racial discrimination). Hansard. HC Deb 15th May 1963, Vol.677, cc149-150w.
89 *Bristol Evening Post* 1 May 1963 and 2 May 1963.
90 *Bristol Evening Post* 3 May 1963.
91 *Bristol Evening Post* 3 May 1963.

networks made much of not only employer opposition but also rank and file opposition to Nethercott's 'no colour bar' public announcement. Busmen and bus-women were interviewed and their views were, in the main, unashamedly hostile to the introduction of black workers. One white bus conductress said, "We don't want them at all. No, no, far too much trouble." Another conductress remarked, "I would not like to work with them at night." When asked the reason by the TV interviewer, she replied," I don't know, there's just something about them." In 2023, at a 'Pride of Britain' awards ceremony, Guy Bailey was shown this film footage. He commented that, "My heart moans, moans, every time I see these pictures. I shed tears inside, it's hard to live with".[92]

Bus driver Mr Ted Neale said,

> The TGWU is wrong in thinking we will support the West Indians ... Mr Ron Nethercott, the union's regional secretary, is barking up the wrong tree in thinking there is no opposition over employing coloured labour.[93]

Mr Cyril Buckley, BOC traffic manager, said in a TV interview,

> ...we are as such at the present time operating a colour bar, simply because, whilst we can within this city, we shall go on employing white labour before coloured labour.[94]

In response to these views by both bus crews and management, demonstrators held an impromptu meeting on Broad Quay, where Paul Stephenson told the crowd of more than one hundred:

> We want equality. They manage it on the buses in Bath, where there are about ten coloured people employed and the white people are quite happy about it.[95]

An *Evening Post* article by John Alexander headlined, 'Coloureds man buses in Bath' stated that black men were working as bus crew in Bath, twelve miles from Bristol. The Bath bus company was a subsidiary of the BOC. The photo with the article showed friends, 'Snowball' Cumberbatch and 'Maverick' Bright—nicknames they gave each other—bus crew in Bath, reading about Bristol's 'Colour Bar War' in the *Western Daily Press*.[96]

92 Pride of Britain: A Windrush Special. ITV programme on 19 October 2023.
93 *Western Daily Press* 2 May 1963.
94 BBC television and Round Up, BBC Home Service, 30 April 1963
95 *Western Daily Press* 2 May 1963.
96 *Bristol Evening Post* 1 May 1963.

Nethercott refused Paul Stephenson's offer to meet with him, on the grounds that he was "unrepresentative".[97] He then adopted the age-old tactic of divide and rule by persuading Bill Smith, a local black TGWU member and chair of WIA, to sign a statement with the union which called for "sensible and quiet negotiations" to solve the bus dispute. However, this backfired as the WIA publicly called: "upon Mr Nethercott not to use Bill Smith as a stooge in this affair".[98]

For its part, whilst "reaffirming the union's national policy of opposing racial discrimination in any form", the union publicly accused Paul Stephenson of, "jeopardising the welfare of the city's coloured citizens" and deplored, "the situation which had arisen as a result of Mr Stephenson's campaign".[99] Nethercott went further and launched a personal attack on Paul Stephenson in the *Daily Herald* newspaper (a Labour Party organ) calling him "dishonest and irresponsible".[100] Paul Stephenson sued both the newspaper and Nethercott for libel and the case later went to the High Court which, in December 1963, awarded him damages and costs. An open apology was given to him by both Ron Nethercott and Odhams Press, the newspaper's owners.[101]

The Bristol Council of Churches led by Oliver Tomkins, Bishop of Bristol, launched a mediation attempt to identify the 'true' leader for the black people in Bristol. The Bishop had previously publicly declared that Paul Stephenson was "a troublemaker". On Friday 3rd May, the church leaders issued a statement blaming both sides for the conflict:

> We seriously regret that what may prove to be a racial conflict … has apparently been created by a small group of West Indians professing to be representative. We also deplore the apparent fact that social and economic fears on the part of some white people should have placed the Bristol Bus Company in a position where it is most difficult to fulfil the Christian ideal of race relations.[102]

This was not the Christian ideal that Stephenson and other activists had expected. Martin Luther King Jr had received active support from the churches and Stephenson had expected the same. In reaction to the church leaders' statement, WIDC members marched from St Paul's to picket St Mary Redcliffe Church after Sunday morning service when worshippers were leaving.

97 *The Times* 6 May 1963.
98 *Bristol Evening Post* 6 May 1963 and *The Times* 7 May 1963.
99 *Western Daily Press* 4 May 1963.
100 *Daily Herald* 4 May 1963.
101 P. Stephenson and L. Morrison, *Memoirs*, p.59.
102 Reported in the *Bristol Evening Post* 3 May 1963.

Peter Carty, a WIDC member, recalled, "we then decide to march to Redcliffe Church … and we … get up there and stand out there at the side of the road and have our protest".[103] Most of the 80 to 100 marchers were black people in work. Madge Dresser commented that this "may well have been the first black-led march against racial discrimination in Britain".[104] This significant protest was covered the next day by the local press with a small but inaccurate piece in the *Evening Post*.[105] Paul Stephenson reported in his memoirs that the radio coverage of this particular protest also underestimated the number of demonstrators.[106]

At the May Day rally held on Monday 6th May in Eastville, members of the Bristol Trades Council publicly criticised the TGWU for its position, and TGWU officials were personally lobbied to take a more vigorous stand against the colour bar. One Trades Council member there at the time recalled,

> there was a great deal of barracking of the TGWU … The TGWU appeared in a very poor light because they had a mass demonstration of local people here criticising them in public.[107]

The campaign against the colour bar led to one of the largest mailbags that the *Evening Post* newspaper had ever received. Contributors wrote in support of both sides of the issue. Some letter writers worried about England drifting into the type of prejudice "rife in South Africa" or "the Southern states of the USA which are a blight on the name of civilisation".[108] Some letter writers expressed overt racist views whilst some white Bristolians were prepared to speak out publicly against the colour bar. TGWU member and long-time activist J.E. Flowers wrote a letter asking,

> How can TGWU officials in Bristol repeat on May Day the worldwide appeal 'Workers of the World Unite!' unless they oppose the ban on coloured workers by the Omnibus Company?[109]

Another supportive letter by 12 local people, who signed themselves the 'Good and the Great of Bristol', stated, "We deplore the fact that West Indian citizens are being refused employment as bus crews in Bristol. We hold

---

103 M. Dresser, *Black and White*, Peter Carty interview, p.31.
104 M. Dresser, *Black and* White, p.31.
105 *Bristol Evening Post* 6 May 1963 and picked up by national dailies, *Daily Telegraph* 6 May 1963, p.19 and *The Times*, 6 May 1963, p.8.
106 P. Stephenson and L. Morrison, *Memoirs*, p.60.
107 M. Dresser, Black and White, Don Bateman interview, p.31.
108 *Bristol Evening Post* 7 May 1963.
109 Mr J E Flowers letter to *Bristol Evening Post* 1 May 1963.

that this is an act of discrimination against Commonwealth citizens".[110] The signatories included Fenner Brockway MP who was, at that time, campaigning in Parliament for legislation to be introduced banning racial discrimination. Some bus crews were supportive and an *Evening Post* article, headlined 'A petition to support West Indians', reported,

> Bus crews are among 200 people to have signed a private petition condemning BOC. They are drivers and conductors who use Hartcliffe Community House canteen.[111]

The direct personal intervention of the two High Commissioners was to prove pivotal to the campaign at this point. Sir Learie Constantine, a popular former cricketer, turned diplomat, had published a pamphlet nearly a decade before called *Colour Bar*.[112] The opportunity for intervention presented itself when Constantine visited Bristol to watch the West Indies cricket team play Gloucestershire in early May. He had already written to the BOC, but while he was at the Bristol match, he made a statement to the press criticising the company's policy, pointing out that at the nearby town of Bath, the same company did not impose such a ban. Constantine expressed moral indignation about the colour bar:

> For it to be happening in Bristol of all places is even worse when you remember that the West Indian sugar industry has helped, through the slaves sent by this country, to make Bristol great.[113]

After an unsuccessful private meeting with Bristol Lord Mayor, Alderman Leonard Stevenson,[114] he decided to go straight to the national leadership of both union and bus company. Constantine met with Frank Cousins, national chairman of the TGWU, who, at that time, was arguably one of the most powerful men in the country. Constantine argued, "I knew his union was against the colour bar … so it was clearly a matter of asking them to enforce their own conviction".[115] Crucially, he also went to the BOC's parent company, the Transport Holding Company, which had ultimate control over BOC management. He persuaded them to send officials to talk with the union. The company chairman told Constantine that racial discrimination was not company policy.[116]

110 *Bristol Evening Post* 2 May 1963.
111 *Bristol Evening Post* 2 May 1963.
112 L. Constantine, *Colour Bar* (Stanley Paul: 1954).
113 *Western Daily Press* 6 May 1963.
114 Ald. Leonard Stevenson had been a member of the Joint Transport Committee.
115 G. Howat, *Learie Constantine* (London: Allen and Unwin, 1975.) p.187.
116 G. Howat, *Learie Constantine* (London: Allen and Unwin, 1975.) p.188.

Laurence Lindo also held discussions with Sir Philip Warter and Sir Reginald Wilson, the chairman and director of the Transport Holding Company. This meeting resulted in Warter and Wilson disavowing Bristol's bus company colour bar policy. Both men gave Lindo their public and 'unqualified assurance' that their subsidiary company in Bristol would end its discriminatory practices. Lindo accepted that the Holding Company had previously issued a general policy directive of no discrimination but that, "this had been ignored in Bristol".[117] One of the senior officials of the Holding Company was sent to Bristol to conduct "very delicate negotiations" between BOC and the union.[118]

Such was the national prominence of the boycott, the BOC and TGWU were forced to engage in negotiations, albeit without the involvement of the WIDC. Within a week of Ian Patey meeting with his London superior, Patey publicly appealed to 'his' busmen for "a real gesture of goodwill in the colour bar dispute".[119]

Whilst the local press congratulated Patey on his swift and effective response, both local papers scolded union leaders for their 'cool' one. The *Evening Post* editor said:

> What a pity the union response, so far at least, has given the impression of being cautious and reserved. A little more warmth and generosity of spirit would not prove nearly so lethal as some union leaders seem to imagine.[120]

Even though the Transport Holding Company had stressed that the colour bar was in breach of its employment policy, the Bristol Bus Boycott campaign lasted a further four months as secret negotiations between BOC and the union continued. It is not publicly known what occurred during those weeks of negotiations as no news was reported until a mass meeting of 500 of the city's 1,750 bus crews reached agreement on 27th August 1963, for "the employment of suitable coloured workers as bus crews".[121]

On 28th August 1963, Ian Patey announced in a joint statement that, "There will now be complete integration without regard to race, colour or creed. The only criterion will be the person's suitability for the job".[122] The settlement of the bus dispute was widely reported in both local and national newspapers.

117 *Western Daily Press* 8 May 1963, The Times 8 May 1963.
118 *Bristol Evening Post* 8 May 1963.
119 *Western Daily Press* 14 May 1963.
120 *Bristol Evening Post* 14 May 1963.
121 *The Guardian* 27 August 1963, *Bristol Evening Post* 28 August 1963, and *Western Daily Press* 29 August 1963.
122 *Bristol Evening Post* 28 August 1963.

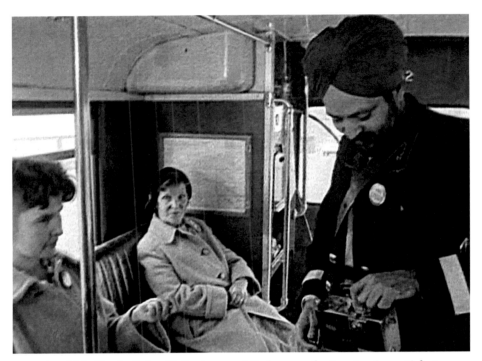

Raghbir Singh, Bristol's first non-white bus conductor, issuing a ticket.

This was coincidentally on the same day that Martin Luther King made his famous 'I Have A Dream' speech at the March on Washington in America. On 28th August 1963, 250,000 black and white Americans showed their support for civil rights for all by marching to the steps of the Lincoln Memorial. Originally the march was for 'Jobs and Freedom' but the goals were expanded to include demands for the passage of a Civil Rights Act. How fitting then that this event coincided with the lifting of the colour bar by both the BOC and the local union branch in Bristol.

On 17th September 1963, Raghbir Singh, a Sikh, became Bristol's first non-white bus conductor. A few days later two Jamaicans, Norman Samuels and Norris Edwards, and two Pakistani men, Mohammed Raschid and Abbas Ali, joined him. Norman Samuels later became Bristol's first black driver in October 1964 and on his first day, crowds gathered to see him.[123] However, over two years later, there were only four drivers and 309 conductors from ethnic minorities in Bristol's total bus crew. Could the ending of a colour

123 Vernon Samuels speech at the Bristol Bus Boycott celebration at the M Shed Museum on 28 April 2023.

bar have been replaced by the imposition of a colour quota? Madge Dresser commented that one former branch official recollected that, "the upshot of the thing was that it was agreed that 5% of the staff could be engaged as (coloured) conductors." Another company employee asserted that the quota was raised to 6% by the early 1970s.[124]

For many years, the success and influence of the Bristol Bus Boycott campaign was neither publicly remembered nor recognised. Whilst the US Montgomery Bus Boycott is indelibly etched onto global memory, a similar fight against racial injustice in Britain is largely forgotten. It was not until the 50th anniversary of the event that the Unite union, the successor union to the TGWU, issued an apology for the union siding with the bus company. A group of trade unions in South West England funded a reprint of Madge Dresser's booklet, with a new foreword.[125] In 2014, a commemorative plaque was unveiled inside the rebuilt Marlborough Street Bus and Coach Station. It took until December 2022 for six leaders of the campaign to be awarded the Freedom of the City.[126] Barbara Dettering, the only female activist amongst those honoured, commented:

> It was a hard struggle. It was a daily struggle. Many times I skipped work, luckily I wasn't sacked, to be at a meeting of some sort where we were planning the next move—and thankfully it paid off.[127]

She attributed the success of the campaign to the black community pulling together:

> I saw a group of people doing something for themselves and I wanted to be part of that. We stuck together in those days, through thick and thin.[128]

She described herself as one of the "silent diggers", working away in the background to support the male leaders of the campaign.[129]

---

124 M. Dresser, *Black and* White, p.48. Also, BBC Teach Series, *Black British Stories: Vernon Samuels— The Bristol Bus Boycott of 1963*.
125 Dresser's pamphlet remains the seminal work on the Bristol Bus Boycott. M. Dresser, *Black and White* reprint edition 2013.
126 The six were Guy Bailey, Barbara Dettering, and Roy Hackett; Owen Henry, Prince Brown and Audley Evans were given the honour posthumously.
127 Bristol Live, 14 December 2022.
128 In conversation with Barbara Dettering on the Bristol Bus Boycott guided walk on 30 September 2023.
129 In conversation with Barbara Dettering on the Bristol Bus Boycott guided walk on 30 September 2023.

The solidarity of the many unnamed men and women who supported the campaign was crucial to its success but is barely remembered. In 2023, Amirah Cole, former Labour Councillor for Ashley Ward, rightly paid tribute to them by commenting:

> The boycott would not have achieved its aim without the full support of the community. A personal example being my dad, who walked from Avonmouth to Montpelier every day as he refused to break the boycott by getting the bus. The boycott was a shining example of solidarity and what people can achieve when they stick together to campaign against injustice.[130]

The Bristol Bus Boycott campaign was more publicly marked in Bristol by a range of events to both commemorate and celebrate its 60th anniversary.[131] Up until this time, the narrative of the Bristol Bus Boycott had tended to focus on the WIDC male leaders and the experiences and contributions of black female activists underrepresented. However, during and after the 60th anniversary events, black female activists became visible and their stories began to be heard.[132] Joyce Morris-Wisdom's account in this publication is the first to be published.

Legislation

The Bristol Bus Boycott was one of the most strategically organised campaigns against racial discrimination in twentieth century Britain. Paul Stephenson believed that "it was the most important thing, because it was the first major struggle that black people had around the civil rights issue, the right to work without discrimination".[133] The campaign raised the issue of racial discrimination on a national level, not only in employment and the trade unions but also in other aspects of life. The boycott helped to challenge official complacency about racial injustice in Britain. It influenced the first anti-discrimination legislation in the form of the Race Relations Acts of 1965 (public spaces) and 1968 (housing and employment).

In 2015, a parliamentary debate recognised this influence. David Lammy, MP for Tottenham, said:

130 *Bristol Evening Post* 17 November 2022.
131 Julian Davis, founder of Curiosity UnLtd, organised many events in 2023 to honour the Bristol Bus Boycott activists.
132 Unite film *Bristol Bus Boycott Pioneers: The Lost Voices,* 2024. Three female campaigners tell their stories: Joyce Morris-Wisdom, Tina Johnson and Cherry Hartley, the first black female bus conductor in Bristol.
133 Bristol Black Oral History interview with Paul Stephenson.

...this is also a moment to think of our homebred heroes such as Paul Stephenson, who organised the boycott of Bristol buses because of their refusal in 1955 to employ anyone of a black background; that contributed to our getting the Race Relations Act 1965. This year, we celebrate 50 years since that Act was passed, and I hope Parliament will celebrate that occasion appropriately.[134]

A celebration took place nearly ten years later in 2023, when senior Labour MPs honoured the activists who had taken part in the bus boycott campaign.[135]

The campaign should also be seen in the context of Britain's changing position in the decolonising and post-colonial world. Post-WW2 Britain sought to rebrand itself as a custodian of human rights and 'motherland' of the Commonwealth. The existence of a colour bar on its own soil was highly embarrassing as the accusations of hypocrisy during the bus boycott were well-founded. The Bristol Bus Boycott of 1963 is not only part of Black History but also part of British History. As Roy Hackett stated, "We had a dream. We must be recognised as a British subject not just as a black man".[136]

The Bristol Bus Boycott should be remembered and celebrated as an event that saw black people standing up for their civil rights as British citizens in the employment sector. In doing so, they challenged the institutional racism of both an employer and trade union.

---

134 Hansard.parliament.uk/Commons/2015-10-1/debates/1510216000003/ BlackHistoryMonth?highlight=slave
See Joyce Morris-Wisdom's account of the boycott activists' visit to Parliament in August 2023 where she was shown a copy of the original Race Relations Act 1965.
135 Milan Perera, 'Westminster honours the leaders of the Bristol Bus Boycott at special event' *Epigram* 25, October 2023.
136 *Remembering Roy Hackett*, a special report from ITV news, ITV West Country 14 December 2022.

From left to right, Roy Hackett, Tony Benn, the Lord Mayor, Paul Stephenson and Guy Bailey at the 40th anniversary celebrations of the Bristol Bus Boycott.

"I Was There!" — My Story by Joyce Morris-Wisdom

You may write me down in history
With your bitter, twisted lies,
You may trod me in the very dirt
But still, like dust, I'll rise.

Maya Angelou, *And Still I Rise.*

The year, 2023, marked the 60th anniversary of the Bristol Bus Boycott campaign which I took part in as a fourteen-year-old activist. At the time, I did not realise just how significant this campaign would turn out to be. It is only in later years that I've come to recognise that it was the first black-led campaign in the UK against racial discrimination since WW2. Despite it being a watershed moment in the British Civil Rights Movement, many people still do not know about it. I hope my personal account will contribute to raising awareness of this important event in British history.

I was born in Jamaica, where my father emigrated from to work in England, as a fighter pilot for the British Royal Air Force in WW2. A career he loved and was very proud to be part of an elite institution in 'Our Mother Country'. I had two siblings, and I was the middle child. Sadly, my brother passed away at the age of four. At the end of the war, my father returned to Jamaica, but came back to England and settled in Bristol. He was one of those who answered the call from the adverts when England asked, yet again, for help to rebuild the country and put it back firmly on its feet. He worked on amphibious military vehicles that operate both on land and water.

My mother followed my father to England in the 1950s and because of her caring nature and being inspired by Mary Seacole, she pursued a career in nursing. She worked as a State Enrolled Nurse (SEN) at Ham Green Hospital, Pill in Bristol. During this time, my sister and I stayed with our aunt until my parents sent for us. This was the norm in those days. In 1962, aged 13 years old, I came with my sister to England in an aeroplane. I mention this because many people assume that my family came on the SS Empire Windrush ship. We never heard of this ship or any other one for that matter. My sister also pursued a career in nursing like our mother. She worked as an SEN at Stoke Park Hospital in Bristol which specialised in providing care for individuals with learning difficulties.

I went to Baptist Mills Secondary Modern School, where I was in a class with predominantly African descendant/Caribbean children, some of my peers were four years older than me. We were never taught about the history

Note on terminology

I don't use the word Black and white simply because the word 'Black' is a political term and people are people, like a bouquet of flowers with different colours from different parts of the world. I can't remember ever being asked how I would like to be referred to or what word would make me feel comfortable with the colour of my skin. So, it's African descendant for someone who looks like me and I refer to other people as Europeans, Dual Heritage and Asians.

of slavery, racism or colonialism. At school, they never told us the truth about our ancestors or the European idea of their supremacy towards African descendants in Africa and the Caribbean. I often wondered why people asked us why we were in this country, as if we did not belong. So, when I was told to go back to my own country, I told them that although this was not my country of birth, this was my home too—we were here to stay.

We were taught mostly English not African-Caribbean Literature so we read books like *The 39 Steps* by John Buchan and plays like Shakespeare's *Romeo and Juliet*. Other childhood stories which we read included *Ukulele and her New Doll*, and poems such as Longfellow's *The Story of Hiawatha*. I was particularly impressed by Miguel De Cervantes's novel *Don Quixote* who believed that people should "dream the impossible and find the courage to reach the unreachable". His stories were about striving against the toughest challenges and winning through to the other side, despite whatever the world might throw at you to put you off-course. This belief had a profound effect on me and influenced the way I've lived my life.

These were the same books that we had read in Jamaica, so the British Education system did not serve me well. It was like the 'Jug and the Mug' theory. The teachers were the educators and we were the passive recipients who must take what was given to us—like a teapot and cup. The only thing I liked about school was the morning break when we had jam doughnuts and cold milk. What I liked about school in Jamaica was reading children's stories like the famous *The Little Red Hen* and the *Rumpelstiltskin Story*. My favourite reading was the African Ashanti/Ghanaian folk tales, introduced by the Maroons[137] in Jamaica, about a character called Bro Anansi, the clever trickster spider. What

137 Price, Richard (ed) *Maroon Societies: Rebel Slave Communities in the Americas* Johns Hopkins University Press, 1996)

I really missed about Jamaica was feeling free, unlike in Bristol where I am continuously being referred to as black, like an object i.e. a black dog, motor vehicle, clothing or a sofa. I was also referred to as brown or a minority ethnic person, or even worse being called a scrounger or being treated like a second-class citizen.

I joined Baptist Mills Youth Club, which was in Bean Street, only a street away from my school. I went with my European friends as a form of protection as there was a constant fear of the Teddy Boys who were known for being abusive and dangerous towards people of African descent. I was a volunteer helping in the tuckshop. Paul Stephenson was the youth leader at the Youth Club, and he knew my parents. The 1960s was a time when people of African descent and Asian people experienced overt racism. We lived in a hostile environment where we couldn't get a safe and decent place to live because of the signs in the windows saying "NO BLACKS. NO IRISH. NO DOGS", and although the British government invited us to come here, they made no preparation to accommodate us on our arrival. This experience did not have a positive impact on us.

Due to the institutional racism in the UK banking system, people arriving from the Caribbean were often unable to access bank services and loans to buy their own homes. Jamaicans drew on their own strengths and resourcefulness, and, being a very close-knit community, they formed a weekly Pardner plan. A Pardner plan was and still is a traditional Jamaican method of saving in which several people pool funds by contributing a fixed sum of money over a specified period.[138] The accumulated sum is then withdrawn by each person based on an initial agreed period of time. This is a simple and quick way of collecting money for big financial expenses like buying a house. The Pardner scheme is like a rotating savings club, except you aren't paid interest and is based on a verbal contract of trust. My mother was the treasurer for our local Pardner plan which gave every member the opportunity to purchase their first house.

There were everyday instances of racism. European people did not want to sit beside us on the buses. This meant that because they were not always sitting properly on their seats, when the bus went round a corner, the Europeans passengers almost fell off their seats. I laughed inwardly seeing this because I feared what might have happened if they realised that I was laughing at them. Many European people had a fear of touching our hands in the shops, it seemed as though they thought our colour would rub off on them. We had to put our money on the counter and our change was likewise put on the counter. There

138 https://www.bankofengland.co.uk/museum/online-collections/blog/community-savings-and-the-pardner-hand

Joyce and one of her friends, Valerie Porter, in Mina Road Park.

was overt racism in employment too. Both my parents experienced it, although my father spoke little about the hostile reception he experienced except to say, "he felt physically sick that at a time when everyone was fighting to stay alive and restoring peace, he could be looked at with so much hate".

My mother also talked about how she was told, "do not touch me" and was shouted at by patients saying, "take your Black hands off me". She also said that they spat on the floor and told her to clean it up and she experienced racist comments like, "go back to your own country." My sister experienced less hostility from the patients with learning difficulties, simply because, she said, "the patients appeared to appreciate being cared for and did not harbour such hostile, racist views." She did comment that "some of the nurses and other members of staff would continuously ask why did you come to this country, why don't you go back to where you came from, we don't want you here, but at the time I did not comment because I felt proud of my chosen profession, and it was not about scoring points about the colour of mine and their skin". People of African descent, men in particular, had difficulty getting a job through no fault of their own. I had a strong sense of justice and equality because of my upbringing and education. Even as a schoolgirl, I felt that it was important to stand up against the racism and discrimination that we were facing in British society.

In April 1963, I heard about Guy Bailey, a young Jamaican man, being denied a job interview with the Bristol Omnibus Company simply because of the colour of his skin. I decided to become an activist and so joined the campaign to stop the 'colour bar'. In order to join the protest marches, I asked my mum's and my teacher's permission to be absent from school. Due to the very close-knit community where we lived and my mother being a close friend of Ena Hackett, Roy Hackett's wife, my mother felt that I would be looked after whilst marching in public spaces. I knew that she felt worried for me, but she couldn't join the march because of her work commitments. I was glad for the chance to take part in the campaign, as I felt it was a unique opportunity to take a stand for what I believed in. However, I also had mixed feelings. As a teenager, I was excited, yet not sure if I should take part. I started to think about what I would do if there was trouble on the streets, where would I run to and who would help me. Obviously, if there was trouble, the men would not be able to ensure the safety of us all. However, despite being only fourteen years old, I felt mature enough to join the marches and the sit-ins. I reflect on this now, and realise that, as a teenager back then, I did not fully appreciate the potential grave dangers that I was facing and how it could have impacted me both then and afterwards.

I carried a placard with words to the effect, 'NO RACISM HERE'. The marches were organised in such a way that us youngsters and women were on the inner lines with the men on the outside. This arrangement was intended to provide us some protection, should we be attacked either verbally or physically, especially by the Teddy Boys who were constantly wanting to attack us. My greatest fear was the uncertainty of the situation. We were committed to non-violent action, but we couldn't be sure of the reaction from the public or the bus crews whilst we were out on the streets. We didn't know how we would be received because the media coverage of events in the American Civil Rights Movement showed very hostile reactions towards the protesters by many people of European descent. I wondered if the same could happen in Bristol as the campaign was getting lots of local media attention. We had European allies joining us and, in particular, some university students arranged a march in solidarity on May Day. Whilst the solidarity march of mainly European students received plenty of publicity in the media, our march to Redcliffe church got virtually no coverage, despite being led by people of African descent. After four months of protests, the bus company and the Transport and General Workers Union (TGWU) local branch finally gave in. On 28th August 1963, the bus company announced that the colour bar would be lifted.

I felt proud to have been part of a peaceful campaign and my parents were pleased with the outcome too. They felt, like me, that it was the right thing to do not only for ourselves and our community, but also for the wider community of Bristol. Although my parents felt more comfortable going about their daily lives, they were still mindful that there could potentially be attacks from some of the public who were angry at the success of the campaign. They praised me for being so brave, particularly because of my age and were thankful to the elders for ensuring I got home safely. I could hardly believe what I achieved but felt good that I had had the courage to take part. Who would have thought at the time that our campaign would change the course of history? Our successful actions would greatly influence the introduction of Race Relations laws which would benefit everyone in the UK. My dream came true, "the impossible became the possible". In my later years, I have reflected on why the campaign was so successful. For me the strength of the African-Caribbean community at that time was critical, our shared belief in seeking justice, fairness and equality. The intellectual and charismatic leadership provided by Paul Stephenson was central to the campaign's success. Also, we were supported by European allies, in particular Mr Anthony Wedgwood-Benn and Bristol University students.

When I left school, I was encouraged to take up a career in nursing but I declined because I didn't feel that it was the right profession for me. However, I did forge a career in the 'caring' professions. Initially, I trained to be a Youth Worker and became Bristol's first woman of African descent to lead and work with young people in Bristol. I also pursued further education and training in health and social administration which enabled me to work as a civil servant for the Department of Health and Social Security (DHSS), the Probation Service and then as a social worker in Children and Families Services. Raising a family, studying and working were challenging at times but it was worth it, as I felt that I was making a difference to the lives of Bristol citizens.

The Bristol Bus Boycott campaign and its legacy remained forgotten for many years. When I retired, I was determined to actively record details about this struggle for racial justice in collaboration with some of the other activists involved. Over the years, I have shared my experience of being a young activist of African descent in the campaign, through radio interviews and talks in schools. The talks were, and still are, to raise the profile of this 'hidden history'. My wish that all schoolchildren should learn about the campaign led me to be involved in an oral history project in 2011. My interview in the Bristol Bus Boycott documentary can be found on vimeo.[139] Also, in 2015, I attended an event with Paul Stephenson, Roy Hackett and ex-mayor of Bristol, George

139 https://vimeo.com/45846316

Ferguson, to launch a resource pack about the campaign which was circulated to all Bristol schools. I still feel that it is important that school children know about this history and a campaign should be launched to get the Bristol Bus Boycott to be taught as a core subject in the national curriculum.

Although there were no great celebrations to mark the 50th anniversary, I was especially delighted to be asked, in 2022, to be involved with a theatrical musical production of the Bristol Bus Boycott performed in Birmingham. The musical was called *To The Streets* and I was the inspiration for the character called 'Lorraine'.[140] I was pleased that the production team wanted to do a piece where the central character was a young woman of African descent who found her voice. The story of the Bristol Bus Boycott was told from her perspective rather than the usual one of the five male leaders. I was invited to take part in a programme of activities to both commemorate and celebrate the 60th anniversary of the Bristol Bus Boycott. Telling my story at a number of events made me realise just how brave we activists were—taking on, not only the bus company but also the union. A highlight was being invited to Parliament by a Bristol MP, Thangam Debbonaire, to see a copy of the first Race Relations Act of 1965. I was one of three surviving activists, together with descendants of the five leaders, supporters and some young people who were learning about the campaign for first time, who were able to see and hear from parliamentarians, how the campaign had influenced the first anti-discrimination legislation in the UK.

It took until the 50th anniversary for Unite union (successor union to TGWU) to formally apologise for its behaviour during the campaign. However, it was not until October 2023 that this union honoured the activists at its first-ever National Black History Month awards gala in Birmingham. I felt really honoured to have won a Unite award and at the awards ceremony, I proudly proclaimed, on behalf of the activists, "We changed the course of history." Our/my dream was to end the colour bar on the buses and we made it a reality.

The Bristol Bus Boycott was an important moment in British history—it's not just Black history or Caribbean history, it's *British* history and should always be remembered as such. The fight for racial justice is not over, there is still racism in British society. In the 1960s, it was overt racism, but later it became more hidden, and thus more difficult to challenge. Sadly, the events in Bristol on 3rd August 2024, have shown the return of overt racism and fascism.

---

140 https://chinaplatetheatre.com/whats-on/in-development/to-the-streets/

Bibliography

Archives

Bristol Archives
Bristol Archive Records https://www.bristolarchiverecords.com
Bristol Anti-Apartheid Movement Archive Papers Collection
Bristol Transport Joint Committee Minutes of meeting 15 March 1962.
Bristol Transport Joint Committee Minutes of meeting 20 May 1963.
Hackett, Roy Archive Papers Collection Ref no 43743/2/1 Vol 1. 1963-1970.
Roy Hackett interview, https://www.bristolarchiverecords.com/people/people_Roy_
  Hackett.html
Stephenson, Paul, Archive Papers Collection of Newspaper cuttings
Stephenson, Paul. Tape 52 Paul Stephenson, Part 1 (1997). BROFA/0132
Stephenson, Paul. Tape 52 Paul Stephenson, Part 1 (1997). BROFA/0133

Bristol Central Library Reference Section
Black Oral History Project, G. Bailey Interview transcript. 1995.
Black Oral History Project, Paul Stephenson Interview transcript. 1995.
Coloured Population of Bristol, 1961-1973—Collection of Newspaper Cuttings. Ref.
  no. B28496. Location RL2E1.

University of Bristol Special Collections
Nonesuch Magazine
Nonesuch News

UK Parliament Commons Hansard Archives
Government report—The Stephen Lawrence Inquiry Report of an inquiry by Sir
  William Macpherson.
Home Office CM 4262-1. Published 24th February 1999.

Newspapers and Periodicals

Bristol Evening Post
Daily Herald, The
Epigram University of Bristol independent student newspaper
Gleaner, The,
Guardian, The
Paris Review, The
Socialist Worker
Times, The
West Indian Gazette
Western Daily Press
Western Mail

Books and Articles

Achebe, C. 'The Art of Fiction', *The Paris Review*. No.139. Winter 1994

Agard, S. A. and C.Carroll, *The Bristol Bus Boycott: A Fight For Racial Justice* (London: Collins BIG CAT, 2022). A book for children.

ANC, *From Unity in Action: A Photographic History of the ANC*, South Africa 1912-1952 (London: ANC, 1982)

Angelou, M. *And Still I Rise* (London: Virago Press, 1992)

Benn,T. *Out of the Wilderness Diaries, 1963-1967* (London: Hutchinson,1987)

Brah, A. *Cartographies of Diaspora: Contesting Identities* (London: Routledge, 2005)

de Cervantes, M. *Don Quixote* (London: Penguin Classics, imprint 2018)

Coard, B. *How the West Indian Child is made Educationally Sub-Normal in the British School System* (New Beacon Books, 1971)

Crawford, E., *The Bristol Bus Boycott 1963*. Dissertation Swansea University. 2019.

Dabydeen, D., J. Gilmore & C. Jones, *The Oxford Companion to Black British History* (Oxford: Oxford University Press: 2007)

Davison, R. B., *Commonwealth Immigrants* (London: OUP, 1964)

Deakin, N. *Colour Citizenship and British Society* (London: Panther Books,1970)

Dresser, M. *Black and White on the Buses: The 1963 Colour Bar Dispute in Bristol* (Bookmarks Publication, 2013—reprinted from the 1986 original with a new foreword)

Du Bois, W.E.B. *The Souls of Black Folk* (London: Penguin: 1996)

Fryer, P. *Staying Power: The History of Black People in Britain* (London: Pluto Press, 1984).

Grant, C. L. *Ukulele and Her New Doll* (New York: Little Golden Books/Simon & Schuster, 1951)

Howat, G. *Learie Constantine* (London: 1975)

King Jr, M.L. *Stride Toward Freedom: The Montgomery Story* (New York: Harper and Row, 1958)

King Jr, M.L. *Why We Can't Wait* (New York: Harper and Row,1964)

McDermott, G., *Anansi the Spider: A Tale from the Ashanti* (New York: Henry Holt & Company Inc, 1987)

Malcolm X Elders Forum. *Our History: Many Rivers to Cross* (Bristol Community Education, UWE and The Beacon Centre, 2003)

Marsh, C. *The Beloved Community: How Faith Shapes Social Justice from the Civil Rights to Today* (New York: Basic Books, 2006)

Mason, P. *Learie Constantine* (Oxford: Signal Books Ltd,2008)

Perry, K.H. *London is the Place for Me: Black Britons, Citizenship and the Politics of Race* (Oxford: Oxford University Press, 2015)

Ramdin, R. *The Making of the Black Working Class in Britain* (Hants: Gower Publishing Company Ltd: 1987)

Sullivan, W. 'Black Workers and Trade Unions 1945-2000' in *Britain at Work: Voices from the Workplace 1915–1995*, TUC Library Collections, London Metropolitan University 2012

Stephenson, P and L. Morrison, *Memoirs of A Black Englishman* (Bristol: Tangent Books, 2011)

Williams, J. *Eyes on the Prize America's Civil Rights Years,1954-1965* (New York: Viking Penguin Inc,1987)

Websites and website articles

J. Kelly 'What was behind the Bristol bus boycott?' BBC News, 27/8/2013, https://www.bbc.com/news/magazine-23795655 (Accessed 21/3/2023).

T. Mazumdar, 'What was behind Bristol bus boycott?' Newsnight, 28/8/2023, https://www.bbc.com/news/av/uk-23863577 (Accessed 21/3/2023).

BBC Teach Series, Black British Stories: Vernon Samuels—The Bristol Bus Boycott of 1963. 2021.

Bristol Museums 'The Bristol Bus Boycott Stories' 2019.
https://www.bristolmuseums.org.uk/stories/bristol-bus-boycott

https://hansard.parliament.uk

https://socialistworker.co.uk/features/how-we-organised-to-break-racism-on-bristol-buses 8 October 2013

TUC 150 years Bristol Bus Boycott: Bristol's forgotten civil rights scandal. https://www.tuc150.tuc.org.uk

Bristol Bus Boycott documentary https://vimeo.com/45846316

Picture credits

Inside-front cover, top—BRHG.

Inside-front cover, bottom—Courtesy Joyce Morris-Wisdom.

Page 17, left—*Western Daily Press*, 1st May, 1963. Copyright Reach plc.

Page 17, top-right—*Bristol Evening Post*, 30th April 1963. Copyright Reach plc.

Page 17, bottom-right— Courtesy Available Light Productions.

Page 18, top—Courtesy Available Light Productions.

Page 18, bottom—Courtesy Available Light Productions.

Page 29—Courtesy Available Light Productions.

Page 33—Bristol Archives 43609/Ph/22/1.

Page 37—Courtesy Joyce Morris-Wisdom.

Acknowledgements

I am indebted to Madge Dresser whose pamphlet both inspired and informed my own research. Special thanks to Joyce Morris-Wisdom and Guy Bailey for sharing with me with their eyewitness accounts of the campaign. I am particularly grateful to Dawn Dyer, Bristol Central Library, for making the library's collection of newspaper cuttings of this historic event readily available to me. My appreciation goes to Barbara Segal and Trish Mensah for reading early drafts and offering helpful advice. Richard Grove's excellent graphic work has enhanced the publication. Huge appreciation goes to Richard Musgrove for skilfully coordinating the whole publication process and providing useful guidance throughout.

Silu Pascoe

A big thanks to all members of Bristol Radical History Group involved in the production of this publication. I am deeply appreciative to Silu Pascoe for supporting me to tell my story.

Thank you to my sons for their support, advice and computer technical knowledge which helped make this pamphlet possible.

Special thanks go to Guy Bailey whose experience sparked the bus boycott campaign and whose friendship has endured.

Karen Garvey (Bristol Museums) and Madge Dresser were particularly helpful to me in keeping the memory of the campaign alive. I am indebted to Steve Preddy, Regional Secretary, SW Region, for his efforts in the Unite union to publicly honour the Bristol Bus Boycott activists.

My story is dedicated to Dr. Paul Stephenson and all the other pioneer activists of 1963.

Joyce Morris-Wisdom